The **Affirmation of Faith Journal** will encourage you to write your own affirmations, goals, prayers, and the things that motivate you. Be purposeful in writing down your goals, be committed to the dreams you have for yourself, and be intentional in working hard no matter what challenges come your way.

As you look forward and beyond:

- Praise God for His goodness every day!

- Live your life on purpose!

- Be grateful!

- Take nothing for granted!

- Give back every chance you get!

- Always Believe in your Dreams!

- Keep a positive attitude!

- Take some self-care time!

- Spend time with family!

- Pat yourself on the back for your many admirable achievements!

- Let no-one, and I mean absolutely no-one limit your dreams!

- If you Believe, you will Achieve!

First Printing. Printed in the United States of America.
ISBN: 978-0-578-33379-3 (pbk)

Designed & Edited by A2Z Books Publishing Lithonia, GA 30058
www.A2ZBookspublishing.net

Author has allowed this work to remain exactly as
the author intended, verbatim.

Affirmations of Faith Journal

PRESENTED TO:

_____

PRESENTED BY:

_____

THIS JOURNAL BELONGS TO:

_____

DATE:

_____

PSALM 23

The LORD the Shepherd o

A Psalm of David

Affirmations of Faith Journal

Giving God Thanks for His Renewed Mercies

By Reciting Affirmations of Faith Every Morning

Dr. Donna M. Barrett

Name of Press:

City and State:

PSALM 23
The LORD the Shepherd o
A Psalm of David

Dedication

This book is dedicated to Kameisha Johnson (my daughter) and Delbon (Dex) Johnson (my son-in-law), for the many challenges they have encountered but still able to maintain a positive attitude. I thank God for their commitment and dedication to renew their walk with Him. Dex and Kameisha have reminded us to cast all our cares on the Lord because He cares for us. They are an epitome of Job, "even though they slay me, yet I will trust the Lord." I am encouraged through their loving spirit and great attitude, to continue to trust in God.

Dex & Kameisha, may the blessings of the Lord continue to saturate your heart and mind as you continue to experience a closer walk with God.

Also, this journal is dedicated to everyone who wants to experience God's refreshing blessings each morning by reciting the Affirmations of Faith to start their day. The selected Bible verses are meant to direct you in a closer walk with God. As you read the Word, as you contemplate on God's mercies, as you meditate on His goodness, you will be challenged to renew your walk with Him.

Jesus is inviting you to take some time from your busy schedule and delve into the Word. This will strengthen you when you are weak, lift you up when you are down, guide you when you have lost your way and encourage you when you are fearful. He is ready and able to give you a new start if you are willing to accept and believe in Him. We serve a mighty God. Go ahead, say your Affirmations of faith with boldness each morning and be ready to open to God's bountiful blessings.

This Journal was completed with a steadfast commitment that *"I can do all things through Christ who strengthens me."* (Philippians 4:13, New Kings James Version).

Acknowledgements

I give all praise and glory to God for being my Rock and Shield and very present help in trouble. I could not have accomplished so much without His constant love, care, and guidance. I express my sincere appreciation and gratitude to my husband, Philip for his love, kindness, and support through the writing of these Affirmations of Faith from the heart. To my lovely daughters; Kameisha, Nekeisha, and Chante, thank you for believing in me, for cheering me on and reminding me that "If I believe, I will achieve."

To my grand-children; Devon, Madison, Laila, and Kairo continue to grow in the love and admonition of the Lord. To my sons-in-law; Delbon, Malick, and Derek. thank you for your prayers and support. A special thanks to my church family for your constant prayers, acts of kindness and encouragement.

To my entire family, thank you for your unconditional love, words of kindness, and continuous support in everything I do.

A special thanks to Pastor Theophilus Roberts and Pastor Norman Harding for sharing words of encouragement and hope and reminding me to keep my focus on what the Lord has called me to do.

To my amazing friends, thank you for always believing in me and cheering me on. Indeed, this has been an incredible experience. It has taught me that I can accomplish anything I set my mind on as long as I have the will, determination, commitment and tenacity to do so.

My mother taught me to pray each morning before I begin any work. Although she is no longer here, the lessons she taught me has captivated my heart and mind. Each morning, before I begin my work, I pray and ask God for wisdom and understanding. I recite my Affirmations of Faith and thank Him for renewed mercies each morning. I believed He heard my prayers and provided the words to write this journal. Praise God from Whom all blessings flow!

"Therefore, I say to you, whatever things you ask when you pray, believe that you receive them, and you will have them." Mark 11:24 I can do all things through Christ who strengthens me." Phil. 4:13

Dr. Donna Barrett

Table of Contents

Introduction

God has been my Rock and Shield throughout my life. The Word of God has comforted me through some difficult times. These experiences have drawn me closer to God and have given me the confidence to trust His unfailing love. I believe there are others who share the same sentiments. In this journal, I have included special Bible verses that are dear to me. These verses have helped me in my walk with God.

Our hope is that these Affirmations of Faith will inspire, encourage, and motivate you to have a closer walk with God. Carve out your own early mornings with God; read the Word, contemplate on His goodness, meditate on how He has carried you throughout your life, pray without ceasing and accept the wonderful blessings He has for you. As you discover God's amazing grace through Affirmations of Faith, you will experience His refreshing love in many ways. God is ready to help you turn over a new chapter in your life.
Let go and let God!

Affirmations of Faith uses a captivating statement approach "I AM," "I CAN," "I SHALL" to inspire you with scriptural reference(s). These affirmations are important to encourage and inspire you to maintain a positive attitude. Following each Affirmation is a prayer and space to reflect and write what is in your heart.

May the Lord continue to bless and keep you; may He favor you with His blessings, may He encourage your spirit as you grow in His grace and may He inspire you to renew your walk with Him. May these Affirmations be a blessing to you! May you share it with others so they can experience the same blessings!

FAITH

I Am Blessed Through The Holy Spirit
I Am Fearfully And Wonderfully Made
I Am Kept In Safety Wherever I Go
I Am Faithful
I Am Still
I Am Focused
I Am Persistent
I Am Confident
I Am A Believer; I Believe In God, I Believe In Me
I Am Not Worried
I Am Trusting In God
I Am Praying Without Ceasing
I Am Praising God In Advance
If I Believe, I Will Achieve
I Can Remove Walls
I Will Rejoice In The Lord
My Hope Is In The Lord
I Can Do All Things Through Christ Who Strengthens Me
I Am Fasting And Praying
I Am A Prayer Warrior
I Ask And I Receive
I Have Radical Faith
God's Divine Intervention
God Is My Miracle Worker
I Shall Not Be Moved

FAITH

Affirmations to Motivate

Choose 5 Affirmations that Motivate You from the Affirmations List.

1.

2.

3.

4.

5.

FAITH

Prayer Affirmation Calendar

On this calendar add your favorite affirmation, prayer, or scripture.

SUN	MON	TUE	WED	THU	FRI	SAT

I Am Blessed Through The Holy Spirit

I indeed baptized you with water, but He will baptize you with the Holy Spirit.
Mark 1:8

John preached in the wilderness and encouraged the people to be baptized. Many people were baptized in the Jordon River. John explained to the people that he baptized with water, but there is One who is mightier than he who will baptize with the Holy Spirit.

The Holy Spirit was presented to us when Jesus returned to Heaven. The Holy Spirit is our Comforter. He speaks to us in accordance with God's Words. When we are baptized with the Holy Spirit, we are renewed in the presence of God. We are emptied of self and all the distractions around us and we are filled with all the attributes of God.

The Holy Spirit brings unspeakable joy and enables us to see points of light in this dark world. Without the Holy Spirit, we would be lost, everything would be chaotic, and we would be hopeless. Genesis 1:2 makes it clear, that out of the chaos, the Holy Spirit hovered over and brought incredible beauty and order.

Is your life seemingly out of control? Would you like to place things in order? Do you want to experience joy in your life? Are you ready for the infilling of the Holy Spirit? The Holy Spirit is ready to illuminate your life with the love of Jesus. Reach out and accept the Holy Spirit and enjoy a new life in Christ.

I am blessed beyond measure by the power of The Holy Spirit in my life. The Holy Spirit fills me with divine love. He is a gentle friend and a blessed comforter. Although I cannot acclaim that I am a perfect example of everything I have written, I know it is by God's ever-present help and guidance that I strive to become more like Him.

Prayer

Baptize me anew with your Holy Spirit. Remove anything that is unlike You and help me to become a vessel that can be used only for Your glory. Wash me in Your Blood and lead me into Your path of righteousness.
I ask to "hover o' er me, Holy Spirit" and give me joy, hope,
and a new beginning.
Amen.

Journaling Page

Journaling Page

I Am Fearfully And Wonderfully Made

I will praise You, for I am fearfully and wonderfully made; Marvelous are Your works, And that my soul knows very well. **Psalm 139:14**

Prior to the pandemic, I visited Emmanuel SDA Church in Atlanta, Georgia. They had Deacon/Deaconesses' Day. Pastor Harvey was eloquent in his presentation of the Word. His topic was entitled "The Dream Team." He reminded the congregation from the Word of God that we are fearfully and wonderfully made. In fact, he reminded us that although millions of sperms are released during intercourse, only one is needed to create me. Therefore, I am not an accident, or an incident but a gift to the world, a divine work of art orchestrated by God.

Knowing that I am a gift to the world and that I am ordained by God to do His will, I must walk with my head high, with extraordinary exuberance and a pep in my step. I am special by the signature of God in my life. I am created in His image. I am called His daughter. I am bought with an extraordinary price through the precious blood of Jesus Christ. I am significant to Him, not because of what I can do but Whose I am. I see the evidence of God's signature on my life every day. Psalm 139: 13 "For You formed my inward parts; You knitted me together in my mother's womb." I am not a mistake; I am precious in the sight of God. Many people believe that they evolve out of nothing, but that is far from the truth. I am created and designed with a purpose. I am unique and so are you. Hence, I celebrate that I am God's masterpiece, intricately designed to feel and know that I am fearfully and wonderfully made. With God's help, I walk in the purpose He has designed for me.

So be encouraged that you are fearfully and wonderfully made!
You are God's masterpiece!!!

Prayer

Eternal Father, thank You for creating me in Your image. I know and accept Your word that I am fearfully and wonderfully made. You love me with an everlasting love and that brings me peace. I sincerely believe that I am made in the image of God. I am under the umbrella of God's divine protection; hence, I celebrate His goodness towards me. In Jesus's name. Amen!

Journaling Page

Journaling Page

I Am Kept In Safety Wherever I Go

Because you have made the Lord, who is my refuge, Even the Most High, your dwelling place; No evil shall befall you; Nor shall any plague come near your dwelling. **Psalm 91:9**

One of the most assuring words is being safe in the hands of God. The psalmist is reminding us in Psalm 91 that the Lord is our refuge and strength and no evil will befall us when we put our trust in Him. Whatever challenges I experience, I am fully covered by God's powerful hand, I am safe.

I feel safe when I turn on my home alarm at nights, when I set the alarm on my car, and when I ensure that the "Ring" is working. However, those safety devices can be tripped by an experienced intruder. They can break in, steal or hurt me. Let's not put our trust only in man-made devices but place our trust in our Creator and Redeemer. He will ensure no plaques will come near our homes. He will protect us from all harm and danger.

As you safely abide in the presence of God, remember Psalm 91: 1-2 *"He who dwells in the secret place of the Most High shall abide under the shadow of the Almighty. I will say to the Lord, He is my refuge and my fortress; My God, in Him I will trust."*

Prayer

Loving Father, how thankful we are for Your ever-protecting care and for reminding us of the safety we can experience when we come to You. Continue to guide and protect us from the snares of the devil and keep us in perfect peace in the name of Jesus. Amen!

Journaling Page

Journaling Page

I Am Faithful

Let us hold fast the confession of our hope without wavering, for He who promised is faithful. **Hebrews 10:23**

I am faithful to God because He is faithful to me. Rahab knew that the only way she could obtain protection from destruction was to risk everything she had. In order to have faith in God, she had to lose faith in everything else! Faith is believing in someone or something you can't see. (Heb. 11:1). Rahab could have turned the spies in and then benefited from the reward of being the one who captured them. She could have discounted the many stories she heard about the Israelites and their God. But Rahab based her faith not on who she is; a woman of Jericho, a prostitute, a woman living on the outside of the city walls, but Rahab based her faith on who God is – the God who does what He says He will do, who keeps His promises, and who protects and saves His people. And in doing so, Rahab willingly surrendered everything she had to His mercy!

Are you going to say "I AM FAITHFUL!" "Even though I don't know what the test result will be, I AM FAITHFUL!" Even though I did not get that job, I AM FAITHFUL; even though I don't know how I am going to pay my bills, I AM FAITHFUL because I know God got my back, I AM FAITHFUL!

Rahab's faith was honored so much later on in the New Testament – for this is the kind of faith that moves the heart of God. When a person surrenders everything, places everything they know, love, and trust on the line and at the mercy of God, then God marvels at and rewards their faith. This is the kind of faith that can move mountains. The kind of faith that Rahab had is the kind of faith that gives rise to hope no matter what circumstance you find yourself in. It is the kind of faith that lifts you up and carries you through the darkest and bleakest times. For, it is during those times that it isn't always easy to see the light, feel the love, or hear the voice of God! But that doesn't mean that He isn't there!!!

Despite the challenges I face, I AM FAITHFUL that God will come through. My faithfulness is based on His ever-present help. Yes, I AM FAITHFUL!!

Lamentations 3:22-23 *"The LORD'S loving-kindnesses indeed never cease, For His compassions never fail. They are new every morning; Great is Your faithfulness."*

Prayer

Our God and Father, thank You for this excellent example of radical faith. Help me to develop faith, even as small as a mustard seed. Help me to remain faithful even though it appears that there is no light at the end of the tunnel. Enrich me with Your grace. Increase my faith in Jesus's name. Amen!

Journaling Page

Journaling Page

Affirmations to Motivate

Choose 5 Affirmations that Motivate You from the Affirmations List.

1.

2.

3.

4.

5.

FAITH

Prayer Affirmation Calendar

On this calendar add your favorite affirmation, prayer, or scripture.

SUN	MON	TUE	WED	THU	FRI	SAT

18

I Am Still

Be still and know that I am God. **Psalm 46:10**

We live in a world filled with chaos, sorrow, gloom, sadness, hurt, problems, deaths, natural disasters and the list goes on. We live in a world of constant busyness, sometimes we say things like: there are not enough hours in the day, where did the time go or I didn't get to do all I had planned. There are so many things to keep us constantly moving, so many things to do, and so many things that are important. We sometimes have challenges to prioritize; mainly because so many things are important. We are constantly on the go, constantly bombarded with things to do. But there is a profound reminder that God wants us to **Be Still.**

The word "Still" is a translation of the Hebrew word **Raphah**, meaning "to slacken, let down, or cease." The words – Be Still – in the English dictionary mean not moving and be quiet. From a Biblical perspective, these two words take on much greater meaning. "Be still and know that I am God." Psalm 46:10. God is defending His city and people. The Hebrew definition is to stop striving, to let go, surrender. **Psalm 46 begins and ends with God is our refuge.** We can take comfort in letting go and resting in God to provide help, strength and safety.

Assuredly, "Be still" is to surrender because God is in charge. Don't fight your own battle as God doesn't need your help. We are reminded in Psalm 27:14 *"Wait on the Lord, be of good courage, and He shall strengthen thine heart: wait I say on the Lord."*

Do you believe you can be still! Do you have faith that God can help you to be still? Whatever you are going through right now... He will be there for you and with you!!! Remember, nothing takes God by surprise! He will give you the strength to endure your challenges. He will not give you more than you can bear. If He takes you to it... He will carry you through it... No one can block your blessings. Remember, if He opens the door, no man can shut it... If He shuts the door, no man can open it. What a mighty God we serve... It's not so much about what He can do but who He is.

Prayer

Dear Father, we are reminded that You work better when we are still. During the waiting period, You want to refuel, refresh, and reestablish us for Your will. Help us to be still in the midst of the storm, help us to be still during the process as You work in and through us. How thankful we are to have a Savior who looks out for our best interest. Increase our faith, help us to trust You more. In the name of Jesus. Amen!

Journaling Page

Journaling Page

I Am Focused

My son, stay focused; listen to the wisdom I have gained; give attention to what I have learned about life So you may be able to make sensible judgments and speak with knowledge. **Prov. 5:1-2**

As you continue on your journey of excellence, you must remain focused on your goals and dreams. It is not always easy to remain focused, especially when you are bombarded with so many things. Some things you can do to stay focused are:

1. Visualize your goals, know exactly where you want to go.
2. Write down all the things you would like to accomplish in the next five years.
3. Create enthusiasm – do not place any restrictions on your thinking.
4. Make no excuses!!!
5. Be specific and personalize your list by starting each sentence with "I am" or "I will." For example, "I am confident," "I will not be moved by the challenges I experience."
6. Set your heart and mind on what you want to accomplish and remain committed.
7. Pursue your dreams.
8. Listen to your heart, create your own journey, persevere, and stay the course.
9. Create exciting pictures of the future.
10. Set goals, be specific, be clear, be flexible, and be realistic.
11. Overcome every obstacle.
12. Share your goals and dreams with a few people you trust. These individuals will support and encourage you when the going gets tough. Stay focused, remain committed, and keep your eyes on the prize.

As I reflect over this list, I am reminded of just how wonderful our Heavenly Father is. He helps us to stay focused. Make Him the center of your world and watch Him work out everything in your favor according to His will! He is our shield, our hope, and our promised victory!

Prayer

Eternal God, help me to be focused on You and not on my problems, help me to be focused on You and not my circumstances. May the blessing of the Lord continue to saturate my heart and mind so I will remain focused on Him. In Jesus's name, Amen!

Journaling Page

Journaling Page

I Am Persistent

*Let perseverance finish its work so that you may be mature and complete, not lacking anything. **James 1:4***

Persistence is the firm continuance in a course of action in spite of difficulty or opposition. You may be going on to a new job, a new school, perhaps, a new home. You will experience challenges. Don't let the challenges deter you from making strides. You must persevere! Develop the "I can" attitude in everything that you do. Remove "I can't" from your vocabulary, and replace it with "I will," "I can," and "I shall." Make no excuses! You will not have enough time to catch your breath between problems because they come so fast. What you have to do is to PERSEVERE! Lessons are often dressed up as detours or roadblocks, and sometimes as full-blown crises. The secret I've learned to getting ahead is being open to the lessons learned.

Develop the grit and grace to navigate the challenges. This will help you to persevere any challenges that come your way. You must persevere!! You can't give up, you can't quit! The moment you quit could be the moment of your breakthrough. Therefore, stay the course no matter how difficult things may get. Recognize that there will be failures, acknowledge there will be obstacles. The goal is to learn from them!! Persevere and make better decisions!!!

When the real estate market crashed in 2008, I lost a great portion of my investments. The thought of closing my real estate business never came to my mind although many of my colleagues closed their business and went back to a 9-5 job. I persevered!!! I kept telling myself, *"This too shall pass."* I attended every workshop, every training, and every seminar hosted by the real estate board. I got all the tools I needed to pivot to the shifting real estate market. It wasn't long that I became an expert in "Short Sale" and "Real Estate Owned" (REO). My persistence paid off big time. Subsequently, I awarded several contracts to sell foreclosed properties for The Department of Housing and Urban Development (HUD), The Department of Veterans Affairs and Fannie Mae (The Federal Government). Today, I am proof that persistence is a major key element to success.

Continue to be persistent in all that you do!!!

Prayer

Eternal and Most Righteous Father, I thank You for the spirit of persistence. I ask for Your divine intervention in my circumstance. Help me to be persistent in my walk with You. In the Mighty name of Jesus. Amen!!!

Journaling Page

Journaling Page

I Am Confident

Confidence is a vital component in your everyday quest to maintain continuous excellence. Stan Smith stated, "Experience tells you what to do, Confidence allows you to do it."

In 1999, South African President, Nelson Mandela celebrated his eightieth (80th) birthday. For almost 26 of those years, he was confined to a prison cell because of his outspoken views about apartheid. During this time, Mandela's confidence must have been severely tested. His faith, conviction and confidence helped him triumph.
Subsequently, he went on to be elected to the highest office; Prime Minister of his country. Confidence is a habit that can be honed and strengthened every day. As you seek excellence, you will be challenged by fear, worry, and uncertainty. Don't quit, don't find excuses, accept the challenge, stay focused, and persevere. Listen to the words by Nelson Mandela at his inaugural speech. This is a man who was confident in himself.

Our deepest fear is not that we are inadequate.
Our deepest fear is that we are powerful beyond measure.
It is our light, not our darkness that frightens us.
We ask ourselves, who am I to be brilliant, gorgeous, talented and fabulous?
Actually, who are we not to be?
You are a child of God.
Your playing small doesn't save the world.
There's nothing enlightened about shrinking so that other people won't feel insecure around you.
We were born to make manifest the glory of God that is within us.
It's not just in some of us, it's in you!
And as we let our own light shine, we unconsciously
give other people permission to do the same. So, shine your light wherever you go...
As we are liberated from our own fears,
Our presence automatically liberates others.

Confidence is the glue that holds everything together. So be confident in all that you do.

Write Your Own Prayer

_____

_____

_____

_____

_____

_____

Journaling Page

Journaling Page

Affirmations to Motivate

Choose 5 Affirmations that Motivate You from the Affirmations List.

1.

2.

3.

4.

5.

Prayer Affirmation Calendar

On this calendar add your favorite affirmation, prayer, or scripture.

SUN	MON	TUE	WED	THU	FRI	SAT

I Am A Believer; I Believe In God, I Believe In Me

Believe in God, and believe in yourself. When you do both, it will change the entire outlook on your life. When my daughters were growing up, I always told them *"If you believe you will achieve."* I wrote it in their Bible, in every birthday card, in their graduation card, and I even posted it on the refrigerator. I think it was etched in their heart and in their minds because now when they give me a Mother's Day card, birthday card or graduation card, they put these same words, "If you believe, you will achieve." Follow your passion, write your own story, be a leader, and be authentic.

A few days ago, my 7-year-old granddaughter, Madison, sent me a text, "Grandma, I was watching a show and the lady said to the other lady, you must believe in yourself. That is good, right, Grandma... I believe in myself! Isn't that the same thing in your book **"Believe?"** I responded right away, *"Yes dear. First, you must believe in God then believe in yourself. If you believe, you will achieve."* She said Grandma, mommy tells me this all the time. I said, "That's great!"

I want you to say after me... "If you believe, you will achieve."

- Believe God's promises are sure.
- Believe that the sky is the limit.
- Believe hard work will pay off.
- Believe you can.
- Believe in your abilities.
- Believe there is light at the end of the tunnel and stay the course.
- Believe in your dreams.
- Believe you can accomplish anything you set your mind to.
- Believe there are always opportunities for growth.
- Believe that adversity is a part of your journey.
- Believe that God is good, He will carry you through the most difficult challenges in your life.
- Believe your DNA is success, growth, strength, and the incredible will to never quit.
- When all these beliefs seem to fail you, remember *Mark 11:24; "Whatever things you ask when you pray, believe that you receive them, and you will have them."*

Over the years, you have shown commitment to personal growth. Life is about growing and embracing all the opportunities to learn new skills that will propel you to a life of purpose. Although you will continue to experience challenges, I envision you reaching for the stars! I believe you will go on to become anything you want to be, I see you believing that the sky is the limit. I see you believing that God got your back. I see you believing that all things are possible when you believe. Believe that each milestone will bring you closer to the goals you have set for yourself.

Prayer

Dear Jesus, help me to continue to believe in You and believe in myself in Jesus's name. Amen!!!

Journaling Page

Journaling Page

I Am Not Worried

Which of you by worrying can add a single hour to his life? ***Matthew 6: 27***

Proverbs 12:25 tells us that "An anxious heart weighs a man down." The heavy burdens of anxiety offer no real benefits. Jesus highlighted this basic futility when he reminded us, in Matt. 6:27 "Who of you by worrying can add a single hour to his life?" It has been said that worrying is like a rocking chair – it gives you something to do, but it doesn't get you anywhere.

One interesting set of statistic indicates that there is nothing we can do about 90 percent of our worries.

- 40% are things that will never happen.
- 30% are about the past –which can't be changed.
- 12% are about criticism by others, mostly untrue.
- 10% are about health, which gets worse with worry.
- 8% are about real problems that can be solved.

I use to worry, I let go of things I have no control over. I let go, and let God. I know it is not easy but it is possible with God's help. When it comes down to it, worry is really a waste of time. But it is also more than that. Worry is not only futile, it's actually bad for us. Why worry when you can pray?

Prayer

Heavenly Father, thank You for Your Word, which teaches us not to worry. Lead us into Your presence and help us to contemplate on You. Help us to stop worrying about things we have no control over. Help us to find the peace that passeth all understanding. In the precious name of Jesus. Amen!

Journaling Page

Journaling Page

I Am Trusting In The Lord

Trust the Lord with all thine heart and lean not unto your own understanding, in all thy ways acknowledge Him and He shall direct thy path.
Psalm 27:14 *declares:*
"Wait on the Lord; Be of good courage, And He shall strengthen your heart; Wait, I say on the Lord."

Psalm 62:2&5 – God is my Rock and my Salvation; He is my Defense... another translation says, "He is my Fortress, I will never be shaken or I shall not be greatly moved." And one of my favorites is from Isaiah 40:31 "But those who wait on the Lord, Shall renew their strength; They shall mount up with wings like eagles; They shall run, and not be weary; They shall walk and not faint." Psalm 37: 5-7 "Commit your way to the Lord; trust in Him and He will do this; He shall bring your righteousness as the light, And your justice as the noonday... another translation... Your reward will shine like the dawn, your vindication like the noonday sun.

These were some of the scriptures I repeated after the surgeon called and said that they have to take my daughter into emergency surgery. He said, "I can't stay on the phone with you, something is eating her tissues, up her stomach walls and down her leg and we are not sure what it is." I hung up the phone, screamed and said Lord, I leave everything in your hands. I trust You, I believe in You, I worship You!! After seven days in a coma and several surgeries, I am happy to note that the surgeries were successful, and she is doing well. We serve an awesome God!

Whatever challenges you are going through, trust in God to carry you through. He is able to do more than you can ask or imagine.

Prayer

Loving Father, thank You for showing up in times of distress when I cry out to You. You responded in ways that only You can. My trust is unshakable in You. Continue to guide and protect me in Jesus's name, Amen!

Journaling Page

Journaling Page

I Am Praying Without Ceasing

Peter therefore was kept in prison: but prayer was made without ceasing of the church unto God for him. **Acts 12: 5**

Pray without ceasing! "Stay in knee city" was one of the suggestions from the late Sis. Alexander. In the midst of the storm... stay in the ship... in the midst of the challenges... stay connected... in the midst of your problems, "Pray without ceasing." The Lord will take care of your battles. His ear is not heavy, He will hear you, His hand is not short, He can reach you. His voice is calm and reassuring; you will recognize His sweet voice. He wants to be in a relationship with you, why not allow Him... why not "Be Still" He is ready, He is able! No matter what you are going through... stay in the ship... it will toss to and fro... but remain calm.

This seems to show the power of prayer and how it can help not just us in our troubles, but in every area of our lives. It seems to show that uniting in prayer with others has great power.

When my son-in-law Dex had to do a heart valve replacement surgery, I invited family members, church family, and friends to intercede on his behalf. We set up a conference line so that everyone could call in at a scheduled time. We sang, read the scriptures and prayed. At the end of the call, we felt confident that God is in control and that the surgery would go well. The surgery was successful. In fact, one of the surgeons was very instrumental in the creation of the robotic arm that was used in the surgery. God always showed up and showed out. Let us continue to pray without ceasing. He will do what He says He will do. 1 Thess. 5:16 *"Rejoice always, pray without ceasing, give thanks in all circumstances; for this is the will of God in Christ Jesus for you."*

It is not impossible to pray without ceasing. We can do it by intentionally keeping our channels of communication open throughout the day and talking to God. Talk to Him as a friend. Tell Him your likes and dislikes. Ask Him to intervene in your life and help you with the impossible tasks. Give thanks for both small and big things, count your blessings, and celebrate His renewed blessings every morning.

Prayer

Dear God, in those times when I am tempted to give up, I hear the still small voice, continue to pray. Thank You for showing up in my situations. Grant me unwavering faith to pray always whether in good or bad times. Help me to become aware of Your nearness and Your willingness to help me. Saturate my heart with Your loving-kindness. In Jesus name Amen!

37

Journaling Page

Journaling Page

I Am Praising God In Advance

And when he had consulted with the people, he appointed those who should sing to the Lord, and who shall praise the beauty of holiness, as they went out before the army. They sang: 'Praise the Lord, for His mercy endures forever. King Jehoshaphat had a very unusual way of organizing an army: "The king appointed singers to walk ahead of the army, singing to the Lord and praising him for his holy splendor. **2 Chronicles 20:21**

Jehoshaphat's battle plan was to put a choir before the army. Envision this: On one side were the three enemy armies amassed to do battle against Israel... 2 Chronicles 20:22... Three armies... the Ammonites, the Moabites and the Edomites (army of Mount Seir).

Then there was the valley where they were going to do battle.
Then Jehoshaphat said to the people of Judah; *"We're going to take those who sing and make a choir out of you and put you in front of the army as you march into battle."*
There's a very important truth here: The Israelites thanked God in advance for the victory. Praise and thanksgiving are verbalized faith. If you thank God after the fact, that's gratitude. If you thank God before it happens, that's faith. No matter what your situation is, Praise God in advance for what you are going through. When you begin to sing songs of praises and give thanks... when you begin to praise God in advance... you will confuse the devil and he will flee from you.

"Your Deliverance Is In Your Praise." I dare you to shout now like you've got the victory right now. I dare you to start praising God like you're going crazy. You don't have to wait for the battle to be over. You can shout right now. It's time to confuse the enemy, he doesn't even know what is going to happen but he will see the ending of your story so praise God in Advance.

- Start praising God in advance for the blessings that are coming your way right now.
- Sometimes, God's blessings are not in what He gives, but in what He takes away.
- Stop trying to pick up what God told you to put down.
- God will wreck your plans when He sees that your plans are about to wreck you. **38**

Prayer

Our Loving Father, give me peace that passeth all understanding. Give me Your Spirit to guide me. Give me Your thoughts to direct my steps. Amen.

Journaling Page

Journaling Page

If I Believe, I Will Achieve

Therefore, I say to you, whatever things you ask when you pray, believe that you receive them, and you will have them. **Mark 11:24**

This is one of my favorite scriptures. In fact, it is on the signature line of my email. Recently, a real estate agent sent a low offer on one of my listings. I told him that the offer was low and the seller will not entertain such an offer. He said, I know it is low, but I saw the scripture in your signature line and thought, "If I believe, whatever things I ask for I will receive, so I am asking." We both thought it was funny and we laughed. I said "I'm glad you took time to read one of my favorite scriptures, but unfortunately, it will not work with this seller.

Our loving Father is not like us. He is merciful, gracious, and loving. When we pray, we must believe that we will receive what we asked for according to His will and we will receive it.

When my children were growing up, I encouraged them with this affirmation "If you believe, you will achieve." They literally believed in this and I am happy that all three of my daughters are doing very well. They have now shared this affirmation with their own children.

Trust God in the big and in the small things. He will come through when you least expect it. He is always on time, ready to help you. Whatever you are in need of, ask according to His will and He will provide. Ask with confidence and He will answer, seek with assurance and you will find, and knock with persistence and the door will be opened. Believe Him with all your heart, with all your mind, and with all your soul for He can do more than you can ask or imagine.

Write Your Own Prayer

_____

_____

_____

_____

_____

_____

Prayers

Journaling Page

Journaling Page

I Can Remove Walls

You may need walls to fall down in your life! You've been making progress by living in the Spirit and you've been making progress by praying in the Spirit. You've been believing the Word of God and advancing in spiritual victory but now it seems you have come up against a wall or some walls.

Walls – symbolize Barriers, Obstacles, Limitations, and Unbelief. I give God all the praise and glory for these walls in my life. These walls experiences have cemented my faith in God. I praise Him for the strength, courage, and tenacity to burst through these walls. It was only because of His constant love and protection that it was possible.

You may feel like you are up against a barrier, like something is hindering you or an obstacle that is in your way and preventing you from making progress. As a matter of fact, the conditions say you are limited but it's time to shout unto the Lord for your walls to come down. The walls of unbelief, the walls of fear, the walls that are hindering you from getting into the promised land.

The God who has brought you thus far on the way did not bring you to the wilderness to leave you. You are standing on the edge of the Promised Land. Your eyes may not be able to see it but set your spirit to receive it. You are on the edge of your breakthrough, on the edge of your victory, on the brink of receiving the fullness of the promises of God. Your walls are about to come tumbling down!

Prophets and Kings... page 202... God was the strength of Judah in this crisis, and He is the strength of His people today. We are to remember that human beings are fallible and erring, and that He who has all power is our strong tower of defense. In every emergency, we are to feel that the battle is His. His resources are limitless, and apparent impossibilities will make the victory all the greater.

Write Your Own Prayer

_____

_____

_____

_____

_____

_____

Journaling Page

Journaling Page

I Will Rejoice In The Lord

Let us hold fast the confession of our hope without wavering, for he who promised is faithful. **Hebrews 10:23**

"He who hath begun a good work in you will complete it in Jesus's name." This was the scripture a friend shared with me as I struggled with a challenge I experienced. Any problems or challenges you experience, take it to the Lord in prayer. Greater is He that is in me than he that is in the world. Rev. 12:11 "I overcame by the Blood of the Lamb. As I contemplated these Scriptures, I can't help but rejoice in the Lord for what He has done for me, what He is doing and what He will do. It is not anyone that has kept me but my Heavenly Father that has blessed and favored me with His loving kindness and tender mercies. She reminded me that I am a beacon of light in this area. Step out in faith, hold your head high, do not let the devil get to you. God got your back!!

These words came at a time when I needed them most. We serve a wonderful Savior. He always sends the right person with the right words to encourage and bolster my spirit. I will not let negative words or deeds hinder me from working for the Lord. "Continue to trust in His unfailing love. He will never leave you nor forsake you and even though you walk through the valley of the shadow of death, fear no evil because He is with you.

Prayer

Thank You Father, for giving me the opportunity to serve You. Motivate and empower me to do Your will and help me to keep my focus only on You. In Jesus' name, Amen.

Journaling Page

Journaling Page

Affirmations to Motivate

Choose 5 Affirmations that Motivate You from the Affirmations List.

1.

2.

3.

4.

5.

FAITH

Prayer Affirmation Calendar

On this calendar add your favorite affirmation, prayer, or scripture.

SUN	MON	TUE	WED	THU	FRI	SAT

My Hope Is In The Lord

If you are going through trials now, take hope in the fact that almost everyone in the Bible who did great things for God had to endure great hardships. In II Corinthians 11:24-27, Paul recounts many of the difficult circumstances that he had gone through. He received forty lashes. He was beaten with rods, he was stoned, and was shipwrecked. He spent a night and a day in the open sea. He was constantly on the move. He was in danger from rivers, in danger from bandits, in danger from his own countrymen, in danger in the city, in danger in the country, in danger at sea, and in danger from false brothers. He labored and toiled and often went without sleep, and food. He was cold and naked.

Clearly, Paul had suffered greatly for the Gospel. However, God used those circumstances to make Paul more mature and to give him a great love for God and for spreading God's Word. Those times of testing allowed Paul to grow closer to God, qualifying him to be a great witness for Christ. Even though Paul had these challenges, he was not moved by them.

Therefore, don't always beg God to change your circumstances. Instead, view each as an opportunity for God to change you, make you mature and complete – not lacking anything. The hardships we experience in our lives are nothing compared to the wonderful home the Lord prepared for us. Let's use these hardship experiences to draw closer to God. He is willing and able to help us overcome these hardships.

God promised to be a very present help in the time of trouble. Since God's promises are sure, I will continue to praise Him. Trouble and hardships won't last always. Weeping may endure for a night but joy comes in the morning.

Prayer

Oh, Heavenly Father, how thankful we are to have a Savior who looks out for our best interest. Increase our faith, help us to trust You more, help us to stop worrying about the hardships we experience and place our trust in You. Help us to find time to sit at Your feet, help us to pray without ceasing. Give us an obedient Spirit to respond to Your Word. In times of uncertainty, let our faith be larger than a mustard seed. Help us to trust in You daily knowing that You know what is best for us. We are relying on Your mercies and ever-flowing grace. Let us not be moved by our problems, challenges, trials, and hardships, but may we stand firm on Your Word. Amen!

Journaling Page

Journaling Page

I Can Do All Things Through Christ Who Strengthens Me

Philippians 4:13

This is one of my favorite scriptures in the Bible. In fact, how can you not make this scripture one of your favorite, uplifting, soul-stirring, take-on-any challenge in the world promise? Paul wrote this promise during some of the most difficult trials of his life. His past experiences allowed him to write boldly, *"I can do all things through Christ that gives me strength."*

In my pre-dissertation class, my professor told the students that he only knew of one student who completed his dissertation in one year. He said, normally, students take 3 to 10 years to complete it. Immediately, I began to say this scripture, *"I can do all things through Christ who strengthens me."* I knew beyond a shadow of a doubt that I can complete my dissertation within one year, with the help of the Lord. To say the least, it was rough and challenging, and many times I thought of giving up, but the words of Paul came forcefully; yes, you can do all things through Christ. Subsequently, to the completion of the first chapter, one of my brothers passed away. It was extremely difficult to stay focused but with the help of the Lord, I remained steadfast in my studies. During the next several chapters, my son-in-law underwent several surgeries. It was difficult to maintain a steady focus but again, my Lord and Savior was there with me. As I reminiscence on this difficult time, I can firmly say that it was only the grace of God that kept me.

At the end of my dissertation, my youngest brother passed away. Yes, it was an extremely difficult time as I mourned the loss of two very dear brothers in 11 months. Even though I am delighted to say that I completed my dissertation in 11 months, I am aware it wasn't me that did it, but it was accomplished through God's strength. At that moment, I realized that the strength of Almighty God reaches down to our pain, our trials, and intense moments and carries us through when we see no way out. James said it well *"Consider it pure joy, my brothers, whenever you face trials of many kinds, because you know that the testing of your faith develops perseverance. Perseverance must finish its work so that you may be mature and complete, not lacking anything."* James 1:2-4.

We are granted the strength by God to navigate the trials, endure the hardships, and grow during them. Let our faith blossom through these difficult times as we grow in His grace.

Prayer

Eternal Father, give us the strength to carry us through the most difficult times of our lives. We recognized that we cannot do it on our own. Through Your merit, show us Your will and lead us to the Rock that is higher than us. Help us to boldly embrace the Scripture: "I can do all things through Christ that gives me strength."
We pray in the precious name of Jesus. Amen!

Journaling Page

Journaling Page

Fasting & Praying

Biblical fasting is refraining from food for a spiritual purpose. Fasting has always been a normal part of a relationship with God. As expressed by the impassioned plea of David in Psalm 42, fasting brings one into a deeper, more intimate and powerful relationship with the Lord.

When you eliminate food from your diet for several days, your spirit becomes uncluttered by the things of this world and becomes amazingly sensitive to the things of God. As David stated, Deep calls unto deep" (Psalm 42:7). David was fasting. His hunger and thirst for God were greater than his natural desire for food. As a result, he reached a place where he could cry out from the depths of his spirit to the depths of God, even in the midst of his trial. Once you've experienced even a glimpse of that kind of intimacy with our God – Our Father, the Holy Creator of the universe – and the countless rewards and blessings that follow, your whole perspective will change. You will soon realize that fasting is a secret source of power that is overlooked by many.

Once you make that decision to fast, even if it is just for a day, God sees the desires of your heart. He will provide you with the grace to endure and see the breakthrough you need come to pass.

Why Fast and Pray

1. It releases the anointing, the favor and the blessing of God in the life of a Christian.
2. It releases supernatural power – If Jesus could have accomplished all He came to do without fasting, why should He fast? The Son of God fasted because He knew there were supernatural things that could only be released that way. How much more should fasting be a common practice in our lives?
3. Jesus fasted – According to Peter, Jesus is our example in all things. (1 Peter 2:21)4.
4. Fasting and prayer bring you to a place of being able to clearly hear God's will.

Whether you desire to be closer to God or are in need of great breakthroughs in your life, remember that nothing shall be impossible to you. Fasting and prayer is truly the secret source of power.

Prayer

Dear Jesus, help us to fast and pray more for the infilling of the Holy Spirit. Only when we are filled with Your Spirit are we able to do supernatural things. Not by might nor by power but by Your Holy Spirit. Teach us to fast and pray. We desire to be more like You in everything that we do. We love and adore You in the Mighty name of Jesus. Amen!

Journaling Page

Journaling Page

The Power Of Prayer

Now to Him who is able to do exceedingly abundantly above all that we ask or think, according to the power that works in us, to Him be glory in the church by Christ Jesus to all generations, forever and ever. Amen. **Eph 3:20**

Alfred Tennyson, the noted English poet of the 19th century, once made this provocative statement, "More things are wrought by prayer than this world dreams of." Additionally, Paul C. Witt wrote these words about the power of prayer:

"It is awesome to contemplate the physical power of the hydrogen bomb. A few ounces of material, carefully controlled, can exert a power of millions of tons! Properly harnessed, this power can do a lot of damage. But there is a power that far transcends that of the hydrogen bomb. It is immeasurably more important because it is spiritual rather than physical. This power is the power of prayer."

One preacher stated, prayer is a platform for divine intervention. Do you need divine intervention in your situation? You may be going through a difficult time; the loss of a loved one, the loss of your job, health challenges, financial problems, and the list goes on. No matter what difficulties you may experience, know that God is able to do more than you can think or imagine. Reach out to Him in faith. He will grant you the desires of your heart according to His will.

My son-in-law needed a surgery to replace one of his heart valves. My prayer group prayed earnestly for the right team of doctors to conduct the surgery. The surgery went very well! After the surgery, we were told that one of the surgeons on the team was very instrumental in the creation of the robotic arm that was used in the surgery. We serve a mighty God. We are confident that He heard our prayers and provided the right medical team for Dex. Won't God do the same for you!

Prayer

Eternal and Most Righteous Father, we are thankful that we can call on You anytime and You are there to provide for our every need. May we be mindful of the power of prayer and call on You in both good and bad times. May we be careful to give You all the praise and the glory! In Jesus' name. Amen!

Journaling Page

Journaling Page

Affirmations to Motivate

Choose 5 Affirmations that Motivate You from the Affirmations List.

1.

2.

3.

4.

5.

FAITH

Prayer Affirmation Calendar

On this calendar add your favorite affirmation, prayer, or scripture.

SUN	MON	TUE	WED	THU	FRI	SAT

I Ask

Ask, and it shall be given you; seek and you will find; knock and it will be opened to you. For everyone who asks receives; and he who seeks finds, and to him who knocks it will be opened. **Matthew 7:7-8**

God promises to bless those that ask Him. We often miss great blessings because we do not ask God. God wants us to ask for what we want. He will grant our needs according to His will.

A story was told of a woman who bought a steamship ticket from Boston to New Orleans. The cost of the ticket was so high that she brought along a case of crackers and packages of cheese, feeling she could not afford the meals on the boat. All through the voyage, she lived on crackers and cheese. On the last day, she offered to pay for the dinner and was told that the meals had been included in the price of the ticket. She had lived on a meager diet of crackers and cheese throughout her trip because she did not ask about what was included in the price of the ticket.

It is important to ask. Do not assume anything. Be bold in your requests! Be confident in what God can do for you! And be grateful for His responses!

When I was 19 years old, I asked God to open a way for me to go to America. I had no idea how I would get there but I believed God would work it out. I boarded the ship one cool summer night with some new friends, not sure of all the details of my trip. The journey was rough, but I made it to America as a stow-a-away under the bottom of a ship. Often, I reminisce on my journey to America and thank God for answering the desire I had. I continue to ask God, even when it doesn't make sense or when it looks impossible because He makes a way.

Continue to ask and you shall certainly receive.

Prayer

Dear Jesus, thank You for Your promise, to ask and I shall receive! Thank You for Your faithfulness, Your care, and Your protection. I worship You. I glorify Your name. Keep me in Your presence as I grow in Your grace. In Jesus' name Amen!

Journaling Page

Journaling Page

Rahab knew that the only way she could obtain protection from destruction was to risk everything she had. She had to lose faith in everything else, to have faith in God. Rahab could have turned the spies in and then benefited from the reward of being the one who captured them. She could have discounted the many stories she heard about the Israelites and their God. But Rahab based her faith not on who she is – a woman of Jericho, a prostitute, a woman living on the outside of the city walls – Rahab based her faith on who God is. The God who does what He says He will do, who keeps His promises, and who protects and saves His people. And in doing so, Rahab willingly surrendered everything she had to His mercy!

Rahab's faith was honored in the New Testament. She surrendered everything and placed what she knows, loves, and trusts on the line and at the mercy of God. Rahab willingly trusted God with her very life and God marveled and rewarded her faith. The kind of faith that can move mountains.

The kind of faith that Rahab had is the kind of faith that gives rise to hope no matter what circumstance you find yourself in. It is the kind of faith that lifts you up and carries you through the darkest and bleakest times. For, it is during those times that it isn't always easy to see the light, feel the love, or hear the voice of God! But that doesn't mean that He isn't there!!!

That's why Jesus said as recorded in John 20:29: Then Jesus told him, "Because you have seen me, you have believed; blessed are those who have not seen and yet have believed."

You are blessed as Rahab was when your faith allows you to believe what your eyes have not seen! When you trust God because of what you have heard about him and not necessarily what you have personally experienced! That is the Power of Faith

Prayer

Father, thank You for the simple, beautiful story of this very special woman, a woman by every human standard unworthy, and by every divine standard equally unworthy. A woman who should have been judged along with her evil civilization, a prostitute. O Lord, how joyous it is to see that You saved her not because of what she was but because of who she believed in. May we know, O God, that our salvation is by faith and by faith alone, but a faith that can stand the test of time. And, Lord, thank You for giving us even that faith. We bless You for the blood of Jesus Christ, shed for the remission of sin. We thank You, Father that in Christ there is forgiveness, even for the unworthy such as we are. Thank You for this powerful story of Rahab's faith. Help us to develop a faith that moves mountains. Amen.

Journaling Page

Journaling Page

Divine Intervention

For nothing will be impossible with God
Luke 1:37

There is no intervention without intercession. Divine intervention is a sudden movement of God upon our challenge or situation. It is when God fights for you and your enemies destroy themselves; when you don't have to stretch a finger to be a winner (Exodus 14:13-14). It is when God does the unusual and uncommon and you can't explain it.

We need divine intervention when we are edged in with no way out. Jehoshaphat found himself in such a situation where he felt he had no way out. He cried out to God who heard his cry and intervened in his situation (2 Chronicles 18:31).

We also need divine intervention when there is no human solution and we have done everything that can be done. Jesus intervened in a seemingly hopeless situation when Lazarus had died. His sister cried out and Jesus intervened, bringing Lazarus back to life (John 11:40).

I experienced divine intervention at several times in my life. I knew beyond a shadow of a doubt that I was safe through His divine intervention; when four gunmen robbed me at my home, when I was hit by a cement truck on the highway and when my daughter almost died after she was diagnosed with flesh-eating bacteria in the hospital.

Whatever situations we find ourselves in, we need to cry out to God, our Father for divine intervention. He is the only One who will answer our prayer and do only what He alone can do.

Prayer

Dear Jesus, thank You for sending divine intervention when I am in trouble. I am grateful that You specialize in difficult situations. Without You, I can do absolutely nothing. With You all things are possible. Only through Your divine interventions, Your divine mercies and Your divine grace are we able to stand. In the name of Jesus. Amen!

Journaling Page

Journaling Page

My God Is A Miracle Worker

God did extraordinary miracles through Paul, so that even handkerchiefs and aprons that had touched him were taken to the sick, and their illnesses were cured and the evil spirits left them. **Acts 19: 11-12**

It was Sunday, December 16, 2018, when the Lord placed in my spirit that my granddaughter, Madison should do a video to let the world know that her daddy is in desperate need of a kidney. I wrote out exactly what Madison should say in the video and texted it to my daughter, Kameisha. You see, my son-in-law, Dex, had severe kidney failure and had been on the donor's list for the past four years. He suffered daily (his kidneys were only functioning 10%). As a result, he had dialysis treatments four times per week and he was in constant pain, muscle cramps, and exhaustion. Everyday his body was deteriorating, and he needed a miracle. God is in the miracle-working business and I believe He will work a true miracle.

Madison created a video with the help of her mom, Kameisha. She posted it on social media and the video went viral. In a few days, my daughter received a call from CBS46 for an interview. Subsequently, the family was contacted by Headline News #CNN for an interview. After both interviews, over 60 people responded to the call to be a donor for Dex. Throughout the next several months, Kameisha kept saying to me, "mom, I think the donor will be David."

On August 26, 2019, David gave Dex the ultimate gift of life, a kidney. It has been two years since the surgery. Dex is recuperating very well. Truly, this was a miracle from God.

Our situation may look very bleak. It may seem that God is not listening, but He always comes through on time. Yes, it may not be our timing, but He is on time. Thank You Lord for choosing David to be Dex's donor! A true blessing and a true miracle!!

Prayer

Eternal Father, we praise and magnify Your name for being our Rock and Shield and a very present help in times of trouble. Keep us in perfect peace while our mind is stayed on You. Save us according to Your loving kindness and tender mercies. May we continue to talk about Your goodness. In Jesus' Holy name. Amen.

Journaling Page

Journaling Page

I Shall Not Be Moved

When I was a little girl, I often sang "I shall not, I shall not be moved, I will be like a tree planted by the rivers of water, I shall not be moved." It has been a long time that I haven't sang that song, but in my heart, beyond a shadow of a doubt, I know that I shall not be moved by the challenges I experience.

It is, as if, sometimes we forget that God is bigger than the situations in our lives. We refuse to move on with what God says as if He is not Alpha and Omega, the beginning and the end, the author and the finisher of our faith. We allow our fear of the unknown and uncertainty to paralyze us and limit us from receiving all that God has planned for our lives. So today, say, "Today is the day that the Lord has made. I will rejoice and be glad in it. I Shall Not Be Moved."

To help maintain the "I Shall Not Be Moved" attitude, speak these affirmations into your life every morning and see how God will show up and show out! These affirmations of faith, give us fresh resolve to handle any challenges that come our way.

I AM BLESSED COMING IN AND BLESSED GOING OUT
I AM HIGHLY FAVORED
I AM A CHILD OF THE KING
I AM FORGIVEN
I AM JUSTIFIED
I AM SANCTIFIED
I AM A NEW CREATURE
I AM A PARTAKER OF HIS DIVINE NATURE
I AM REDEEMED FROM THE HAND OF THE ENEMY
I AM ABOVE AND NOT BENEATH
I AM LOVED BY GOD
I AM NOT MOVED BY WHAT I SEE
I AM HEALED BY HIS STRIPES

Prayer

Dear Lord, help me to maintain an "I Shall Not Be Moved" attitude. I will Praise God despite whatever challenges I experience. Praise God for the victory that has already been won. I will stand firm and not be moved! There is nothing too hard for God. In times of trouble, when it seems like nothing is going right... When it seems like all hope is gone... when it seems like you are down to nothing... this is the time God shows up. In Jesus' name, Amen!

Journaling Page

Journaling Page

About the Author:

Dr. Donna Barrett is a real estate consultant, founder, and CEO of National Fund for Foster Children, author of "Believe," co-author of "Devotionals from Women to Women," philanthropist, and productivity coach. Donna resides in Florida with her husband, Philip. She has three beautiful daughters and four amazing grandchildren. She loves to give back and hopes to engage others to do the same. Her desire is to be a beacon of light wherever she is and walk in the purpose God has designed for her.

Be encouraged by a few of her favorite Scriptures:

"I can do all things through Christ who strengthens me." Phil. 4:13

"Therefore I say unto you, whatever things you ask when you pray, believe that you receive them and you will have them." Mark 11:24

"For I know the plans I have for you declares the Lord, plans to bless you and not to harm you, plans to give you hope and a future." Jer. 29:11

Be encouraged – Be inspired – Be motivated!!!

Made in the USA
Columbia, SC
03 March 2022

56732602R00070